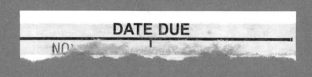

BACH'S Goldberg Variations

Anna Harwell Celenza

Illustrated by
JoAnn E. Kitchel

ini Charlesbridge

Published by Charlesbridge
85 Main Street, Watertown, MA 02472
(617) 926-0329
www.charlesbridge.com

Library of Congress Cataloging-in-Publication Data
Celenza, Anna Harwell.
Bach's Goldberg Variations / Anna Harwell Celenza ; illustrated by JoAnn E. Kitchel.
p. cm.
Summary: Eighteenth-century composer Johann Sebastian Bach helps young organist Johann Gottlieb Goldberg
by giving him lessons and by presenting him with a composition which came to be called the *Goldberg Variations*.
Includes historical notes.
ISBN 1-57091-510-5 (reinforced for library use)
1. Bach, Johann Sebastian, 1685–1750—Juvenile fiction. 2. Goldberg, Johann Gottlieb, 1727–1756—Juvenile fiction.
[1. Bach, Johann Sebastian, 1685–1750—Fiction. 2. Goldberg, Johann Gottlieb, 1727–1756—Fiction.
3. Music—History and criticism—Fiction.] I. Kitchel, JoAnn E., ill. II. Title.
PZ7.C314Bac   2004003301
[E]—dc22
Printed in Korea
(hc) 10 9 8 7 6 5 4 3 2 1

Illustrations done in watercolor and ink on Arches cold press paper
Display type and text type set in Operina, Giovanni, and Della Robbia
Color separations, printing, and binding by Sung In Printing, South Korea
Production supervision by Brian G. Walker
Designed by Diane M. Earley

To Dominic Barth. Thanks for
being a great editor.~A. H. C.

For David and Ford, a couple
of night owls.~J. E. K.

On a cold autumn morning in 1737, Count Keyserlingk sat in a wooden pew at St. Mary's church in Gdansk, Poland. The Count's friend and music adviser, Johann Sebastian Bach, had brought him there, promising a special treat.

"What in the world do you expect to show me here?" asked the Count, shivering. "All I see is a drafty church with a few old parishioners."

Bach pointed to the organ loft above. "There he is. I knew he would come. This is what we have been waiting for."

The Count looked up as a ten-year-old boy sat down in front of the organ. Within minutes, waves of glorious music poured down from the pipes above.

"Who is that young man?" whispered the Count, impressed.

"His name is Goldberg," replied Bach. "Johann Gottlieb Goldberg."

"He has talent!" said the Count.

Bach nodded. "He is good, but not as good as he could be. It is a pity he will never get the training he needs."

"What do you mean?" asked the Count. "Why not?"

"Goldberg is an orphan," said Bach. "He has no one to take care of him."

"Then I shall take care of him," declared the Count, proud of himself for being so generous. "I have been looking for someone to polish my silver and help in the kitchen. I will give him a position at court. There he will be able to earn his keep, and in his spare time he can play the harpsichord in my salon."

Bach did not say anything at first. He had hoped the Count would take young Goldberg under his wing, but not as a houseboy. "Since you are being so generous," said Bach, "I will make an offering as well. Each time I come visit you at court, I will give the boy a music lesson."

"Splendid!" said the Count. "It appears we have both done our good deed for the day."

So Goldberg went to work at the Count's palace in Dresden. Every morning and evening he helped in the kitchen, and in the afternoons he spent hours polishing the Count's silver.

There was little time for music, but Goldberg was not discouraged. His new music teacher, Mr. Bach, gave Goldberg a lesson three or four times a year. Mr. Bach was very kind to him. Goldberg was determined to become a great musician, and he tiptoed into the salon every night and practiced the harpsichord while Count Keyserlingk slept.

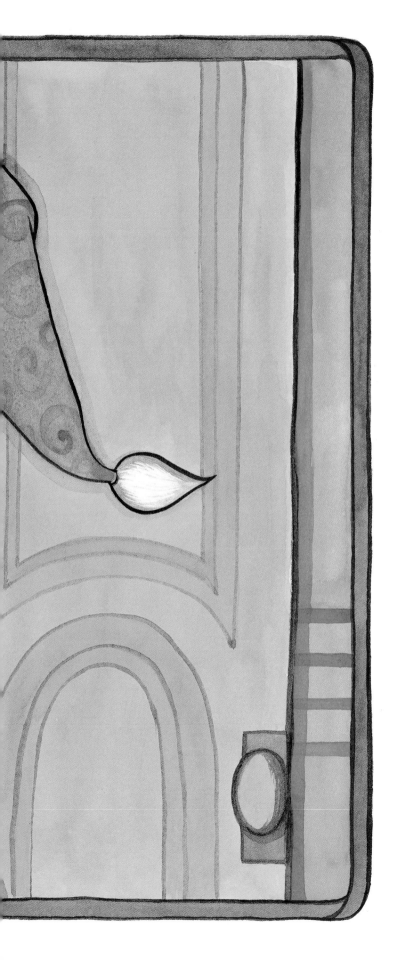

Life continued on like this for several years. But then in 1741, Count Keyserlingk began having stomach pains. He found it hard to sleep. As he lay in bed one night, he thought he heard music coming from the salon. "Who could be playing at this time of night?" he wondered.

Goldberg was so absorbed in his music that he never heard the *tap . . . tap . . . tap* of approaching footsteps. The door slowly opened—*creak . . .* Goldberg stopped playing and cautiously turned around.

"Count Keyserlingk, sir, what are you doing here?" he asked.

"I should ask the same of you," said the Count. "It is terribly late."

"Yes sir, I know. But I need to practice," said Goldberg. "Late night is the only time I have for my music. I hope I did not disturb you."

"Quite the contrary," said the Count. "I was tossing and turning when I heard you playing. It is good to know someone else is awake. Continue practicing. I'll stay and listen."

Goldberg grew nervous. He wanted to impress the Count. He played a lively dance tune. The Count tapped his toes.

"Quite nice," said the Count. "Now let me hear more. Play something that makes your heart pound and your fingers race. Play something really difficult."

"I'm sorry, sir. I don't know any pieces like that," said Goldberg.

"Then learn one," said the Count. "I'll be back in a week."

Goldberg searched through his music and found a piece that made his heart pound and his fingers race. He knew the Count would be pleased. He practiced every night.

When the Count returned at the end of the week, Goldberg was ready. He played his new difficult piece. The Count furrowed his brow in concentration.

"Quite nice," said the Count. "Now let me hear more. Play something complex, clever, and fun. Play me a musical canon."

"A canon?" asked Goldberg.

"Yes, you know what I mean," said the Count. "One of those pieces that goes round and round—where one hand begins and the other one follows."

"I'm sorry, sir. I don't know any pieces like that," said Goldberg.

"Then learn one," said the Count. "I'll be back in a week. And forget about the silver—you should spend the afternoons practicing."

Goldberg searched through his music. He found many canons, but none seemed right. So he stayed up late and composed a piece that was complex, clever, and fun. Goldberg knew the Count would be pleased. He practiced every afternoon and every night.

When the Count returned at the end of the week, Goldberg was ready. He played his clever new canon. The Count was thrilled as the music twirled round.

"Quite nice," said the Count. "Now let me hear more. Play something dance-like and difficult and fun. Play me a piece that has *everything!*"

"*Everything?*" asked Goldberg.

"Yes, you know what I mean," said the Count. "A piece filled with dances and difficult runs. It must also have canons and something quite new. A surprise that will trick me—how about a riddle?"

"A riddle!" said Goldberg in disbelief. "I'm sorry, sir. I don't know any pieces like that."

"Then learn one," said the Count. "I'll be back in a week. And forget about the kitchen—you should spend the whole day practicing."

Goldberg searched through his music. But he couldn't find a piece with *everything*. He stayed up late and tried to compose. But he couldn't write a piece with a canon *and* a riddle that was dance-like *and* difficult *and* fun.

Finally, in a desperate state, he went to Bach for help.

"The Count wants a piece with *everything!*" cried Goldberg. "What am I to do?"

Bach opened a cabinet and pulled out a thick folder of music. "Not to worry," he said calmly. "I have written just the piece."

Goldberg stared at his teacher in awe. "How could you have written a piece with *everything*?" he asked.

"I just took a simple tune—an aria to be exact—and changed it every time," said Bach as he sat down at the harpsichord and began playing a slow, lyrical melody. "This tune is called the theme," said Bach proudly. "Listen carefully and you will hear it change."

As Bach continued to play, the theme disappeared, and a lively dance tune took its place above the harmony. "This is called Variation One," said Bach.

"Variation Two is fast and furious." The old man's fingers raced across the keyboard. Goldberg's eyes grew wide.

"Variation Three is a canon," said Bach, slowing down again. "One hand begins, and the other one follows." Bach played on and on. "Variation Four is a dance called the *passepied*. . . . Variation Five is terribly difficult. . . . In Variation Six a new canon appears. . . . Variation Seven is a dance called the gig. . . . Variation Eight makes the fingers fly. . . . Variation Nine goes round and round. . . ."

It seemed there was no end to Bach's special composition. Each variation was a new invention that lined up after the others in a clear, repetitive pattern: dance, difficult, canon—ten, eleven, twelve—dance, difficult, canon—thirteen, fourteen, fifteen—on and on the piece continued. Goldberg thought it would never end.

"What about the riddle?" he interrupted.

Bach stopped playing. "The riddle?" he asked. "Oh yes, of course. The riddle comes in Variation Thirty. I took some silly folk tunes and mixed them all together. See if you can figure it out."

Goldberg listened carefully as Bach began to play again. Recognizing one of the tunes, he sang the words out loud: "I have been away from you so long. . . ."

Then he recognized a second tune and sang: "Cabbage and beets have driven me away. . . ."

Bach stopped playing. "Good job," he said. "You have found the clues. Now tell me if you can solve my musical riddle."

Goldberg thought for a moment. "What has been gone for a very long time—driven away by *vegetables*?" All at once it came to him. He took a seat next to Bach and quickly flipped the music back to the opening page. "The answer to your riddle is this theme!" cried Goldberg triumphantly as he played the aria from the beginning of the piece.

"The theme is the *meat* of your composition—it sustains the whole work—and now it has been gone for a long time—for thirty full variations!"

Bach laughed approvingly at his student's quick wit and then joined him in playing the final phrase of the piece. When they were finished, Bach closed the music and handed it to his student. "You may borrow it, if you like."

Goldberg returned to the palace with the special composition in hand. He knew the Count would be pleased. He practiced every morning . . . and every afternoon . . . and every night.

When the Count returned at the end of the week, Goldberg was ready. He played Johann Sebastian Bach's dance-like, difficult piece with its "follow me" canons and musical riddle. The Count tapped his toes and furrowed his brow. He was thrilled, and he chortled with glee.

"MAGNIFICENT!" roared the Count. "The *perfect* piece!"

And from that day forward, Goldberg spent every hour practicing his music. Count Keyserlingk appointed him the court's official harpsichordist, and whenever he couldn't sleep, he would call into the night, "Goldberg! Play your variations!"

And that's how Johann Sebastian Bach's *Goldberg Variations* got its name.

Author's Note

When we think about classical music, the names of great composers often come to mind. But music history is as much about performers and listeners as it is about composers. The characters in this story really did exist. Count Keyserlingk, a Russian ambassador living in Dresden, first came in contact with Johann Gottlieb Goldberg (1727-1756) in 1737; he was so amazed by the boy's talent that he offered him a position at court, where he was allowed to take music lessons with both Johann Sebastian Bach and his son Wilhelm Friedemann Bach.

J. S. Bach's first biographer, Johann Nikolaus Forkel, reported that in the early 1740s Count Keyserlingk became ill and suffered sleepless nights. During these bouts of insomnia, Goldberg was often called upon to entertain the count with music. Scholars do not know the precise historical circumstances surrounding Goldberg's acquisition of Bach's composition. Some believe Count Keyserlingk commissioned the work; others propose that Bach gave the piece to Goldberg directly. Whatever the circumstances, it is known that Bach visited the count in Dresden in 1741 and that shortly thereafter Goldberg began playing the *Goldberg Variations* for Count Keyserlingk and his friends.

The *Goldberg Variations* is unlike any other piece written by Bach. It is monumental in scope, extremely difficult to play, and unusual for its extended use of repetition. The theme and thirty variations present an assortment of musical styles: some variations are inspired by dance pieces or orchestral genres, while others take the form of a canon or fugue. The final variation, the musical riddle, is a genre called a *quodlibet,* which means "whatever you please" in Latin. It's a humorous collection of various tunes played at once.

Today, some performers play the *Goldberg Variations* on piano. But it was originally composed for the harpsichord, as the piano had not yet been invented. The harpsichord resembles the piano in appearance, but it produces quite a different sound. Whereas the piano's sound is created by small hammers hitting the strings, the harpsichord's sound is created by small hooks or quills that pluck the strings.

When Bach published his impressive set of variations in 1742, he called them *A Keyboard Practice Consisting of an Aria with Thirty Variations for the Harpsichord.* Given the length of this title, we can see why the count's name for the piece, the *Goldberg Variations,* stuck more than 250 years ago and still remains popular today.